Table of Content

Why Fantasy Football Fellowship? 4
How to Use FFF 5

PreSeason: The Fantasy Football Experts 6
PreSeason: Chaos During a Fantasy Football Draft 10
PreSeason: What Happens After Draft Day 14
Week 1: What is Your Perspective? 18
Week 2: Surprising Performances 22
Week 3: Don't Panic 26
Week 4: Why Did I Do That? 30
Week 5: Trade Rejected 34
Week 6: The Setback From Injuries 38
Week 7: Compounding Mistakes 42
Week 8: Counting the Cost and the Waiver Wire 46
Week 9: Trying to Control the Outcome 50
Week 10: Admitting You're Wrong 54
Week 11: Never Giving Up 58
Week 12: Hope to Make the Playoffs 62
Week 13: The Player We're Glad Got Away 66
Week 14: Fantasy Loyalty 70
Week 15: Consequences for Bad Decisions 74
Week 16: Don't Get Cute 78
Week 17: Winning and Receiving Validation 82

FFF Prayer 86
The Top Fantasy Football Player to Own Each Season 87
UNPACKIN' it Resources 88
References 90

**Videos for each session are available on
FantasyFootballFellowship.com**

UNPACKIN' it Ministries, Inc.
P.O. Box 473173
Charlotte, NC 28247

ISBN: 978-0-692-17888-1

Scriptures Marked ESV are taken from the *The Holy Bible, English Standard Version®* (ESV® Copyright © 2001 by Crossway, a publishing ministry of Good News Publishers.

Scriptures marked NIV are taken from the Holy Bible, New International Version®, Copyright © 1973, 1978, 1984 by International Bible Society.

Scripture quotations marked (NLT) are taken from the Holy Bible, New Living Translation, copyright © 1996, 2004, 2015 by Tyndale House Foundation. Tyndale House Publishers, Inc., Carol Stream, Illinois 60188. All rights reserved.

Scripture quotations taken from the Amplified® Bible (AMP), Copyright © 2015 by The Lockman Foundation. www.Lockman.org"

To purchase additional copies of this or other resources
ORDER ONLINE at www.FantasyFootballFellowship.com
WRITE UNPACKIN' it Ministries, Inc.
P.O. Box 473173, Charlotte, NC 28247
PHONE (704) 303-8435
www.unpackinit.com

Printed in the United States of America

Publishing Team:
Author: Bryce T. Johnson
Editor: Darla J. Johnson
Design: Darin Clark (dclarkcreative.com)
Theological Review: Kris Dolberry (krisdolberry.com)

Dedication

To all the wives who patiently, lovingly, and sometimes reluctantly allow their husbands to play Fantasy Football - especially my wonderful wife, Jodi.

To all the Fantasy Football Fellowship husbands - you finally have a legitimate excuse to give your wives for why playing an imaginary game of football is worth your time.

Why Fantasy Football Fellowship?

After being cut from my middle school football team, I quickly realized that playing "real" football wasn't going to be my outlet for competitiveness and comradery. Instead, I'd be spending the rest of my life watching this amazing sport from the proverbial stands and the comfort of my couch.

Thankfully, my high school Young Life leader offered an opportunity to take my passionate football fandom to a whole new level. He invited me to play in my first Fantasy Football league (15 years ago), which turned out to be a game-changing experience. I was able to use my NFL knowledge and fandom in a way that was fun, competitive, and challenging...and went on to win the first league I ever joined!

Now I play in two leagues every year - one with my high school friends and another one with my college buddies. It's not only a blast to compete and win, but more importantly, I have come to value how Fantasy Football connects people and naturally builds relationships. It gives us guys a great excuse to stay in contact and remain involved in each other's lives. One minute my buddy is telling me about his new son and the next minute we're talking about our Fantasy draft! Fantasy Football has provided me community and camaraderie in ways that are hard to find anywhere else. For that I am truly grateful.

We launched UNPACKIN' it Ministries in 2014 and our vision is to see sports fans everywhere following Jesus. Fantasy Football Fellowship is a ministry resource we hope will create a movement of Fantasy owners rethinking why and how they play. We want to leverage Fantasy Football to provide fellowship and accountability while we live out Hebrews 10:24-25: ***"Let us think of ways to motivate one another to acts of love and good works. And let us not neglect our meeting together, as some people do, but encourage one another..."***

Our hope is that as you play Fantasy Football throughout the season, you find fellowship that involves meaningful conversations about faith and life. Our prayer is that your love and faith in God deepens because most importantly, ***"...our fellowship is with the Father and with his Son, Jesus Christ"*** (1 John 1:3). Have a great season and enjoy the FFF experience!

How to Use FFF

The **FFF Playbook** provides content and discussions that allow Fantasy Football owners to build relationships, grow in their faith, and explore relevant topics that encourage and challenge one another.

Here you'll find weekly sessions that take your league from your Fantasy draft/ preseason to the week after the Fantasy Football Championship. Each session includes a Fantasy concept that relates to a real life topic. Also provided are Biblical applications, discussion questions, and challenges for the week. You can start meeting right after your draft (while the preseason is going on) or begin with Week 1 as it coincides with the start of the NFL/Fantasy season.

Videos compliment each session and are available on FantasyFootballFellowship.com.

Acknowledging the uniqueness of each Fantasy League, the FFF Playbook is designed to best fit your particular owners. Some ideas include:

- **League Meetings:** Discuss the weekly topics from FFF in a group setting (in person, on a conference call, or via video chat) with as many members available. Commissioner/leader facilitates the conversation and asks the questions found at the end of each session.

- **Matchup Meetings:** Get together with your Fantasy opponent for the week (get some trash talk going), then dive into the questions at the end of the week's session. Pray for each other throughout the week.

- **Family Meetings:** The FFF Playbook can be used as family devotionals, with brothers, or during a special father-son time.

Other Suggestions:

- You can use the Playbook even after the season starts, but begin with the same week number as it is in the NFL season.

- Meet every other week and combine topics or rotate between league meetings and matchup meetings. Meet before Monday Night Football or Thursday Night Football and watch the first half together.

PRESEASON

"The only true wisdom is in knowing you know nothing."

—Socrates

The Fantasy Football Experts

As we prepare for our upcoming Fantasy Football season, how do we make decisions about which players to pick up, trade for, and add to our lineups? Do we base our selections solely on the football we watched last year? Do we simply choose our favorite players from our favorite teams? How much do we factor in the opinions of Fantasy Football experts?

Heading into my 15th season playing Fantasy Football, there is no question I rely on the firsthand drafting experience I've gained over the years. I also take into account the limitless hours of football I watched last season.

However, in order to have a successful draft and Fantasy season, I listen to the experts and allow their analysis and predictions to help me. They won't be right about everything or know how each player's season will definitely play out, but they spend a lot of time researching and studying in order to share what they learn. It's up to us as Fantasy owners to listen to the wisest and most trustworthy Fantasy experts before making our choices.

This same mentality is even more important with the daily decisions we make and the big decisions we're forced to face throughout life. Knowing our choices can drastically change our course, we can either make them based on our own understanding and perspective...or seek out the advice of those who are wiser than us.

The book of wisdom in the Bible tells us, ***"The way of a fool is right in his own eyes, but a wise man listens to advice"*** (Proverbs 12:15).

Proverbs 11:14 (ESV) says, ***"Where there is no guidance, a people falls, but in an abundance of counselors there is safety."***

We must humble ourselves and recognize we don't have all the answers to our dilemmas, but can greatly benefit by consulting with people who have more experience and expertise in specific areas.

In 1 Peter 5:5 (AMP), Peter writes this to the leaders of the church: *"Likewise, you younger men [of lesser rank and experience], be subject to your elders [seek their counsel]; and all of you, clothe yourselves with humility toward one another [tie on the servant's apron], for God is opposed to the proud [the disdainful, the presumptuous, and He defeats them], but He gives grace to the humble."*

If we truly desire to make wise choices in life, they must be rooted in faith. Proverbs 9:10 is a good reminder: *"Fear of the Lord is the foundation of wisdom. Knowledge of the Holy One results in good judgment."*

If we want to remain in God's will, we must study scripture so we have the proper view of His character and His Word. Also, listening to experienced mentors, pastors, and teachers who have a deeper understanding than we do, can provide valuable insight.

Just as we seek the knowledge of Fantasy football experts for a successful season, let's be aware of opportunities to receive Biblical wisdom from trustworthy people. Let's be wise in all areas of our lives (career, marriage, and parenting), but most importantly in our pursuit of following Jesus. When we stop "choosing players" based on our own limited understanding, we can start taking advantage of the wisdom of others.

Today, let's be challenged by the encouraging words found in Proverbs 15:22 (AMP): *"Without consultation and wise advice, plans are frustrated, but with many counselors, they are established and succeed."*

Prayer:

Heavenly Father, as I desire to remain in Your will, please give me the wisdom to make the right decisions in my life. Thank you for allowing me to pursue wisdom that flows from Your Word. I ask to receive wisdom from reliable experts, counselors, mentors, and advisers that You've placed in my life...instead of trying to figure everything out on my own. I pray this in Jesus' name, Amen.

Questions to Unpack Personally or in a Group:

1. Who or what do you rely on when making decisions in life?

2. What prevents you from asking advice from others?

3. When has good advice protected you from making a bad decision?

4. When didn't you listen to advice or pursue wisdom from an expert and it ended up costing you?

5. What decision or issue could you presently use the advice and wisdom of others? What might prevent you from doing so?

THIS WEEK'S CHALLENGE:

Ask someone in your life to consider being your mentor or ask someone if they'd be interested in you mentoring them.

PRESEASON ✓

Did You Know?

The inventor of Fantasy Football was a contractor named Bill "Wink" Winkenbach who had a minority stake in the Raiders.[1]

Chaos During a Fantasy Football Draft

The Fantasy Football draft is one of the best days of the year! Feeling like you're an NFL general manager and selecting the right players for a winning team is exhilarating. When a player we want is still available and we're able to draft him, the excitement escalates...and getting praise from the other owners for an impressive pick we make is also very satisfying.

Although being with friends and talking football is a lot of fun, there's also a level of chaos and intensity while concentrating on the building of our teams. There's pressure to select great players, find value in those who slip to a later round, and do last minute research for up-to-date information.

We also have to make sure to pursue and listen to trade offers from other owners, keep track of the players already taken, and pay attention to our roster so we don't take too many tight ends.

The stress really kicks into high gear when we're actually on the clock to make our pick. As we look at all of our options, we start to doubt ourselves, go back and forth on who to take, and get nervous about making a mistake. The clock ticks away while everyone waits for us to choose our player. Eventually, we must confidently make a decision and move forward.

In the end, our selections are only for Fantasy Football and the stressful scenario is all in the context of an enjoyable hobby. However, in real life, we often find ourselves in the middle of a stressful, overwhelming, and head-spinning season of life.

When everything is moving at a rapid pace, we can feel like we're "on the clock" and can't keep up with all of the decisions that need to be made and the options that need to be considered. It starts to feel like there is chaos all around us.

Although most of us have these types of challenges from time to time, the truth is that we can't thrive or even survive in the mayhem unless we rely on Jesus for strength and peace. Even when we can't prevent stressful situations, we must remember to pause and invite Christ to get us through.

The following Bible verses provide encouragement for these difficult times in life:

2 Thessalonians 3:16 (NLT) says, *"Now may the Lord of peace Himself give you His peace at all times and in every situation. The Lord be with you all."*

We can repeat this prayer from Isaiah 26:3 (NLT) — *"You will keep in perfect peace all who trust in You, all whose thoughts are fixed on You!"*

Psalm 29:11 (NLT) tells us, *"The Lord gives His people strength. The Lord blesses them with peace."*

When considering our own "draft room" with high gear stress, and situations that cause us to be "on the clock" (nervously going back and forth on what to do so as not to make a mistake), let's remember that Jesus can give us peace and strength to overcome the craziness. Instead of letting the chaos take over, we can confidently rely on Him for wisdom to make a decision and move forward.

Prayer:

Heavenly Father, I find myself overwhelmed, stressed, and exhausted. I can't get through this alone and I need the strength and peace that are found in Jesus. Help me not allow the craziness and chaos of life to take me off course, but instead cling closer to You. Thank you for peace. In Jesus' name, I pray, Amen.

Questions to Unpack Personally or in a Group:

1. How do you normally handle situations that require tough decisions? What is your process?

2. What emotions tend to take over when you feel like you're on the clock?

3. Once you make a decision, what might cause you to doubt yourself or second guess your choice?

4. In your life right now, what situation has you feeling like you're on the clock?

5. How does trusting Jesus help you make confident and clear decisions?

THIS WEEK'S CHALLENGE:

When you feel like you're on the clock or about to make a decision, pause and ask Jesus to give you peace and guidance. Pick one of the verses from the session to memorize and reflect on when you feel stressed.

PRESEASON

Did you know?

The first Fantasy Football draft took place in Oakland, California in August of 1963. [2]

What Happens After Draft Day?

As Fantasy Football owners, we spend all summer preparing for our draft and figuring out which players we want to select. We consider the rookies joining new teams and how quickly they have a chance to contribute, as well as, which players will have the biggest impact after signing with a different franchise in free agency.

We take a look at the players with the best potential for a breakout season, so we can determine which round they should be drafted, and also make sure to cross guys off our list if they're overvalued and have the potential for a disappointing season.

All of this research and the different thought processes involved are centered around the Fantasy draft and the team we assemble to start the season. Obviously, emphasis should be placed on this day, as making the right decisions determines the success of our team's upcoming year.

However, Fantasy Football doesn't end once draft day is over. It's only the beginning of a season filled with roster management, lineup decisions, dropping and adding, trades, and keeping up with NFL news and notes. All of these elements are ongoing throughout the Fantasy Football season.

With that in mind, the most important day in "real life" is the one when we receive Jesus Christ as our Lord and Savior. The moment we decide to surrender and invite Jesus to take over and forgive us of our sins is the day that should be completely and unquestionably emphasized.

The Apostle Paul writes in 1 Corinthians 15:3-4 (NLT), "I passed on to you what was most important and what had also been passed on to me. Christ died for our sins, just as the Scriptures said. He was buried, and He was raised from the dead on the third day, just as the Scriptures said."

This is the good news available to us! When we place our faith in Jesus' work on the cross and receive His grace, we become a child of God for all of eternity.

The day our hearts are changed is a monumental day. We're saved because of Jesus, not because of anything we do. We don't earn salvation based on our works, but our attitudes and desires are transformed when we choose to faithfully follow Him.

Just like Fantasy owners don't stop on draft day, but continue throughout the season, we step into an on-going life with Christ after the day of our salvation.

Colossians 2:6-7 (NLT) says, *"And now, just as you accepted Christ Jesus as your Lord, you must continue to follow Him. Let your roots grow down into Him, and let your lives be built on Him. Then your faith will grow strong in the truth you were taught, and you will overflow with thankfulness."*

The day we surrender is the starting point of a life of faith that includes growth, maturity, and understanding of God and His Word. Just like Fantasy owners are asked to take care of lineups and make necessary changes each week, we're called to a life that is honoring and glorifying to Him.

As we daily take steps of obedience to do what God requires of us, let's rest in His grace and rely on His strength to enable us to handle all of the challenges we face. Let's cling to this prayer Paul wrote in his letter to the Colossian church:

"...We ask God to give you complete knowledge of His will and to give you spiritual wisdom and understanding. Then the way you live will always honor and please the Lord, and your lives will produce every kind of good fruit. All the while, you will grow as you learn to know God better and better" (Colossians 1:9-10 - NLT).

Prayer:

Heavenly Father, thank you for saving my life and showing me grace. I'm grateful for the eternal life I now have because of Jesus. I pray I would continue to grow and obey as I seek to know You better. It's in Jesus' name I pray, Amen.

Questions to Unpack Personally or in a Group:

1. If you have committed your life to following Jesus, what do you remember about the day you were saved?

2. Why is it important to continue to grow in your faith and understanding?

3. What area of your life have you seen the most growth and maturity since that day?

4. What areas of your life do you still need to grow and mature?

5. What prevents you from taking steps to be disciplined in the growth process?

THIS WEEK'S CHALLENGE:

Take an inventory of your spiritual life and determine ways you can practically grow and mature in your faith and knowledge of God daily.

WEEK 1

"If you are the No. 1 draft pick in Fantasy Football, or if you're No. 2 or 3, you take pride and want to uphold that honor that someone has drafted you that high."[3]
—Former NFL running back LaDainian Tomlinson

What is Your Perspective?

The start of the NFL and Fantasy Football season always brings lots of hope and excitement. Although we don't really know what's going to happen, each of us does our best to anticipate which players we think will surprisingly overachieve and which NFL teams will unexpectedly win. Our guesses factor in injuries, team chemistry, and new coaches.

Our personal perspectives on Fantasy Football lead some of us to think that running backs are the key position for winning the league, while the rest of us place an emphasis on having a great quarterback.

Certain Fantasy owners believe it's worth the risk to draft rookies, and some prefer having veterans in their lineup. There are those convinced a specific player is going to have a breakout season, while others have a completely opposite viewpoint.

Part of what makes Fantasy Football so much fun is how owners within a league can think so differently about players and strategies. We all see the upcoming season through a unique lens. Our season will turn out a certain way as a result of our individualized mindset.

What about the lens we use to view things in "real life?" How do we decide what's most important and what we should value? How do we determine when to take risks or when to remain status quo? What do we believe during difficult situations and what do we think of the challenges others face?

Ultimately, it comes down to whether the lens we filter things through is Biblically or worldly based. This reflects how we talk, act, and handle circumstances, and whether or not our minds are focused on seeing things in a way that pleases God.

It's challenging to consider the reality of our daily mindset, and if the Bible, prayer, and our community give us an eternal perspective. Is our fulfillment found in Jesus when we view our day-to-day life and present struggles? Or do we focus on temporary and unfilling things that bring us down?

Our approach to life can get caught up in the temporary, which leads to questions like "Why me?" or "Why not me?" This type of attitude can easily turn to anger, bitterness, materialism, and power.

The more fulfilling option is an eternal perspective rooted in Jesus' love and grace which results in humility, generosity, contentment, and faithfulness.

Colossians 3: 1-2 says, **"If then you have been raised with Christ, seek the things that are above, where Christ is, seated at the right hand of God. Set your minds on things that are above, not on things that are on earth."**

The perspective we choose today determines what our mind is focused on. If it's based on the world's point of view, our main focus is making money at all cost, acting on whatever makes us happy at the moment, and selfishly doing what we want to do.

Alternatively, if our perspective lies in obeying God, we set our minds on things above so our day is filled with compassion, patience, forgiveness, and love.

Philippians 4:8 (NLT) tells us, **"And now, dear brothers and sisters, one final thing. Fix your thoughts on what is true, and honorable, and right, and pure, and lovely, and admirable. Think about things that are excellent and worthy of praise."**

Our perspective on Fantasy Football affects our season, but the perspective we choose each day affects our eternal lives. Since our behavior displays our perspective, we must decide if we want to think and live for the now… or in view of an immeasurable hope that is only found in Jesus.

Prayer:

Heavenly Father, help me realize that fulfillment is found in Jesus and not in the things of this world. I pray my perspective stays rooted in that, so I can pursue humility, generosity, contentment, and faithfulness. Teach me to view my current challenges in light of eternity, and remain filled with peace and hope. In Jesus' name, I pray, Amen.

Questions to Unpack Personally or in a Group:

1. How do you think your perspective on Fantasy is different from other owners in the league?

2. Briefly describe a time when having the wrong perspective caused you to make a bad decision in life?

3. How does your perspective influence how you handle difficult situations?

4. In what ways has your perspective changed over the years?

5. What are your thoughts on the differences between a Biblical and worldly perspective and which one do you identify with more?

THIS WEEK'S CHALLENGE:

If changing your perspective affects a decision you make this week, share with another owner in the league what happened.

WEEK 2

"It's a leather ball in an oblong shape, weird things are gonna happen."
—Joe Bryant from FootballGuys.com

Surprising Performances

Early in the Fantasy Football season, we get a feel for whether players are going to be team contributors from the beginning and burst onto the scene or get off to a slow start. It's always nice when the studs on our roster jump out of the gate right away and confirm why we took them early in the draft.

But every year, there are also players that come out of nowhere and put up big numbers in the first couple of weeks. They are complete surprises (not at all on our radar) and we don't realize their NFL team is going to use them as much as they are.

Although it's a bonus when the surprise players are already on our team, most often they are still available on the waiver wire and we can try to pick them up with the hope that their strong play continues.

When players have early season injuries, the backups get an unpredicted opportunity, as well. Across the board, we can always count on multiple players coming through in huge and unexpectant ways.

When players have surprising performances early on, we can beat ourselves up for not seeing it coming. But the truth is, it's just a reminder of our limited view and understanding of what happens in Fantasy Football. The out of nowhere scoring actually makes it special and keeps us waiting in anticipation.

Likewise, we have a limited understanding of our own future. Often times we experience unexpected blessings and surprises that seem to come out of nowhere. As soon as we think something is going to go a certain way or we're on the verge of giving up, God comes through in a big and powerful way.

Amazingly, God can show up by providing us with a miracle or an unforeseen provision that blows us away. Although we don't always know how He is going to move or when He's going to do something remarkable, we can confidently know that He is able to do the unimaginable.

Ephesians 3:18-20 (NLT) says, *"And may you have the power to understand, as all God's people should, how wide, how long, how high, and how deep His love is. May you experience the love of Christ, though it is too great to understand fully. Then you will be made complete with all the fullness of life and power that comes from God. Now all glory to God, who is able, through His mighty power at work within us, to accomplish infinitely more than we might ask or think."*

We experience great joy when God delivers in times of need and struggle, especially when it's in such a way that is beyond what we could ever see coming.

2 Corinthians 9:8 (NIV) tells us, *"And God is able to bless you abundantly, so that in all things at all times, having all that you need, you will abound in every good work."*

God's blessings come in abundance and remind us of His goodness, faithfulness, and supernatural power. He is the provider of everything we need. According to James 1:17 (NLT), *"Whatever is good and perfect is a gift coming down to us from God our Father, who created all the lights in the heavens..."*

Just as we excitedly wait for the out-of-nowhere scoring in Fantasy Football, we can anxiously anticipate miraculous and extraordinary blessings from God. It's also rewarding and impactful to look for ways to surprise and bless others and allow God to use us as answers to their prayers.

While living in this difficult and unpredictable life, we can rest in knowing we serve a God who is unlimited in power, so *"...the peace of God, which transcends all understanding, will guard [our] hearts and [our] minds in Christ Jesus"* (Philippians 4:7 - NIV).

Prayer:

Heavenly Father, thank you for the times in my life when You showed up in surprising ways and abundantly blessed me. I pray I would live with the assurance of Your power and love and know that the peace You provide transcends all understanding. In Jesus' name, I pray, Amen.

Questions to Unpack
Personally or in a Group:

1. So far this season, who is your most surprising player and why?

2. Which part of the reading stood out to you the most?

3. Describe a time in your life when God came through in a surprising or miraculous way.

4. Describe a time God used you to do something for someone that blessed them in a surprising way.

5. What area of your life do you need a miracle and for God to do exceedingly more than you might ask or think?

THIS WEEK'S CHALLENGE:

Ask God to show you a way to surprise someone with a special blessing.

WEEK 3

"R-E-L-A-X"
— Green Bay Packers Quarterback Aaron Rodgers

Don't Panic!

We're a couple of weeks into the Fantasy Football season and some of us have more losses than wins...a star player out with injuries...or an underachieving top draft pick.

If we're not careful, we can start to worry and make desperate moves - especially if our team's name is at the bottom of the standings. Although negativity can easily take over, we must prevent ourselves from going into the full-on panic mode.

When we stop to take a look at the bigger picture, it will help us stay calm and make wise decisions. Although we may need to make a trade or work the waiver wire, we shouldn't do anything too drastic after a few early losses.

It's also important to take a look at bye weeks, future matchups, and the scoring of other teams in our league, so we can remember there are plenty of games left to turn around the season.

Another factor to consider is trusting our draft picks. If we have proven players on our roster who have gotten off to a slow start, we should be patient and wait for them to get going instead of cutting them loose too early. Rather than give up on our team in week three, we must remain disciplined and confident that our season will move forward in a positive direction.

Of course, there are some Fantasy seasons where everything goes against us and it's just not going to be our year. Even so, the same principles apply to our attitude. We don't want to panic, be foolish, or make desperate moves that end up hurting us even more.

It's easy to see how this scenario in Fantasy can parallel our real lives. There are weeks in a row or entire years when everything seems to go wrong. We experience loss, disappointment, frustration, and embarrassment.

Our decision on how to respond is still the same - we either panic and make impatient, foolish choices or remain calm and hopeful. We can negatively look at our circumstances and be discouraged or look at the bigger picture, trust God, and rely on Him for guidance.

Proverbs 3:5-6 (ESV) tells us to *"Trust in the Lord with all your heart, and do not lean on your own understanding. In all your ways acknowledge Him, and He will make straight your paths."*

Whether in Fantasy Football or life, there's no benefit to being worried or fearful or putting ourselves in panic-mode. Philippians 4:6 (AMP) challenges us: *"Do not be anxious or worried about anything, but in everything [every circumstance and situation] by prayer and petition with thanksgiving, continue to make your [specific] requests known to God."*

If we follow Jesus, He gives us the strength and peace we need to get through any situation. We just have to rely on Him.

2 Timothy 1:7 (AMP) says, *"For God did not give us a spirit of timidity or cowardice or fear, but [He has given us a spirit] of power and of love and of sound judgment and personal discipline [abilities that result in a calm, well-balanced mind and self-control]."*

As we pray for our circumstances to change, our attitude and mindset can remain the same...rooted in peace and hope.

Prayer:

Heavenly Father, as I experience difficult situations and seasons that don't go the way I planned, help me remain steadfast, calm, and trusting. I know I can rely on You for strength instead of panicking. I pray this in Jesus' name, Amen.

Questions to Unpack Personally or in a Group:

1. What panic move have you already made this early in the Fantasy season?

2. What does it say about your faith when you choose to panic and worry in life?

3. What situation in your life is causing you to panic, fear, or worry right now?

4. What tough experience has God given you peace and strength to get through?

5. How does trusting God allow you to have peace and eliminate worry?

THIS WEEK'S CHALLENGE:

When you feel you're about to panic about something, pause and ask God for peace and wisdom to see the big picture.

WEEK 4

"Failure is part of success, an integral part. Everybody gets knocked down. Knowing it will happen and what you must do when it does is the first step back."

–Former San Francisco 49ers Head Coach Bill Walsh

Why Did I Do That?

During the Draft, or at some point during the first few weeks of the season, most of us make a bad decision we quickly regret. Maybe we draft a quarterback too late or go ahead and take an injured running back too early - despite our gut feeling that we shouldn't.

How many of us go back and forth trying to figure out our starting lineup only to realize the highest point scorer is sitting on our bench? Many of us spend our Sundays thinking about the moves we make and yelling at the TV, "Why did I do that?"

Fantasy Football is filled with second-guessing because we constantly have choices to make between lineup changes and waiver wire adds. We routinely question ourselves for passing on certain players and benching the wrong guys.

We also regret picking players with off-the-field issues when their performance is ultimately affected...dwell on the wrong picks made in the 4th round...and kick ourselves for the trade we should never have made.

But the reality is, we can't go back and draft again or reset our lineup from last week. Instead, we can learn from our mistakes and move on to the next week. We can think about our miscues, figure out what we can do differently, and then focus on the rest of the season.

As bad decisions are made in Fantasy and real life, feelings of regret can easily overtake us in both. We all have mornings when we wake up with strong regret and second-guess our previously made actions and choices.

In real life, these feelings can be beneficial if they lead to a deep desire for change and a willingness to learn from our mistakes. Rather than focusing on our regrets, we can find comfort in God's grace by falling to our knees and shifting our attention to the cross of Christ.

As followers of Jesus we know, *"If we confess our sins, He is faithful and just to forgive us our sins and to cleanse us from all unrighteousness"* (1 John 1:9 - ESV).

When we rest in His love, grace, and mercy, we can move forward in repentance and adjust our decision-making in the future. If we desire to avoid regret and truly please God, then we must cling to Him for wisdom and strength to choose rightly.

Even though we grow and mature in our faith, we still make some poor decisions from time to time. But as Paul explains in Philippians 3:12-14 (AMP), *"Not that I have already obtained it [this goal of being Christlike] or have already been made perfect, but I actively press on so that I may take hold of that [perfection] for which Christ Jesus took hold of me and made me His own.*

"Brothers and sisters, I do not consider that I have made it my own yet; but one thing I do: forgetting what lies behind and reaching forward to what lies ahead, I press on toward the goal to win the [heavenly] prize of the upward call of God in Christ Jesus."

If we're too busy beating ourselves up about our mistakes from the past, we miss out on the next exciting things God has in store for us.

Fantasy Football and real life are guaranteed to be unpredictable, frustrating, and exhilarating - all at the same time. We know we can never do everything right, but there's no value in living with regret. Instead, let's genuinely trust in the Lord and seek His will. When we do, we can be assured His path leads to life, truth, joy, and peace.

Prayer:

Heavenly Father, thank you for Your willingness to lead me and show me the right path to take. Thank you for Your grace when I make the wrong choices. Help me not to remain regretful, but instead to repent and depend on You. I pray I would make wise choices as I trust You with all of my heart and truly seek Your will in all I do. I pray this in Jesus' name, Amen.

Questions to Unpack Personally or in a Group:

1. What is your typical reaction when making a mistake or blowing it in Fantasy and life?

2. Why are regrets positive and when do they become negative?

3. Why is forgiveness crucial in moving on from regrets?

4. Why is it a bad idea to give unnecessary power to your regrets and allow the past to bring you down?

5. Do you have past regrets you still hold onto? What prevents you from letting them go?

THIS WEEK'S CHALLENGE:

Ask God to reveal a regret you're holding onto. Write it down on a piece of paper, then light it on fire as a symbol of letting go.

WEEK 5

"I take rejection as someone blowing a bugle in my ear to wake me up and get going, rather than retreat."

–Sylvester Stallone

Trade Rejected

With the first quarter of the NFL season complete, we have a pretty good feel for our Fantasy Football team. We know which players are contributing or struggling, and have a sense about which players are going to get going soon.

As we take a look at our roster, we might see a position in our lineup that is weaker than the others. When we consider our bench, we realize we have more than enough wide receivers, but very little depth at running back. For some of us, we have a great starting quarterback and a strong backup but can only play one of them each week.

In analyzing our team, we come to the conclusion that we need to make a trade - one of the most fun and challenging parts of playing Fantasy Football! We pull up the rosters of other owners and try to figure out which players we want to trade for. If we have extra wide receivers and need a running back, we look for an owner who has extra running backs.

We select which player or players we are willing to part with and put together a package that helps our team. Once we zero in on what the trade should be, we send the owner a trade proposal and hope he also considers the trade beneficial.

While waiting for the owner's response, we know it will be thrilling if the notification comes back with a "yes," but oftentimes we get the dreaded "your trade offer has been rejected."

When our offer isn't accepted, it's a huge disappointment because of all the time we spent on the deal, putting ourselves out there, and counting on the deal to make our team better. Usually, the other owner doesn't want to part with a player or doesn't like what he gets in return, but even a good reason doesn't ease the rejection.

A Fantasy trade rejection is one thing, but a "no" in real life can be truly painful. We can all relate to being rejected or passed on, and feeling the sense of not being wanted or desired.

Often, we are discouraged by the job we didn't get...or disappointed by the person who wasn't interested in us...or frustrated by not getting accepted into a school or group.

But what if we decide not to be derailed by the rejection and see it as protection from someone or something? What if we choose to accept that another "yes" at another time is actually better for us?

Our faith in Jesus allows us to remain hopeful and rest in the truth that we are wanted, chosen, and accepted by the ultimate King. Even when we face rejection in our lives, we can handle it with peace because of the thankfulness and blessings that come from being one of God's children.

The Bible tells us in Ephesians 1:3-6 (NLT), *"All praise to God, the Father of our Lord Jesus Christ, who has blessed us with every spiritual blessing in the heavenly realms because we are united with Christ. Even before He made the world, God loved us and chose us in Christ to be holy and without fault in His eyes.*

"God decided in advance to adopt us into His own family by bringing us to Himself through Jesus Christ. This is what He wanted to do, and it gave Him great pleasure. So we praise God for the glorious grace He has poured out on us who belong to His dear Son."

Although facing tough setbacks is part of life, let's not allow them to get in the way of embracing our eternal hope and faith in the God of the universe who makes a way for us to be with Him. He always welcomes us with open arms!

Prayer:

Heavenly Father, I still have thoughts and pain about the times I've been rejected. Please help me move forward and focus on the reality that You love me and want me. I pray to be filled with thankfulness and peace because of my union with Jesus. In His name, I pray, Amen.

Questions to Unpack Personally or in a Group:

1. What Fantasy trade did you propose and were bummed that it was rejected?

2. How does rejection make you feel in the moment?

3. What is the toughest rejection you've faced in your life and how did you handle it?

4. What rejection in your life are you actually thankful for?

5. If you're a follower of Jesus, how should you respond to rejection?

THIS WEEK'S CHALLENGE:

Think back to the rejection experiences in your life. In your prayer time, reflect on God's faithfulness and thank Him for His protection.

WEEK 6

"I've had my share of injuries throughout my career. It's humbling. It gives you perspective. No matter how many times I've been hurt, I've learned from that injury and come back even more humble."[4]

–Former Pittsburgh Steelers safety Troy Polamalu

The Setback from Injuries

When football players pursue an NFL career, and we sign up to play Fantasy Football, there's an expectation that injuries will occur. Realistically, players are going to suffer minor injuries on a routine basis and may even face a major injury at some point in their career.

When injuries take place, NFL players deal with pain, disappointment, and missed opportunities. It just comes with the territory. We feel similar emotions (to a much lesser degree) when players on our Fantasy team go down and ultimately affect our season.

As Fantasy owners, we try to avoid injury prone players, but we must realize that whenever a player steps onto the field he has the chance of getting hurt. We can't be delusional in thinking our guys will never deal with some sort of injury during the year.

Similarly, in our own lives, we know we're not free from pain, suffering, disappointment, and missed opportunities. God absolutely blesses His children and allows us to enjoy life, but He never tells us we won't experience setbacks and tough situations.

The reality is that we are going to regularly suffer from both minor and major "injuries" throughout our lives. We must learn to properly handle our responses while accepting that "injuries" come with the territory.

Making the decision to follow Jesus isn't so we have good health and lots of wealth, but because we need a Savior and desire to grow and become more like Him. Although we wish we could completely avoid struggles and trials, they actually refine and strengthen us.

When heartache and suffering come, we can cling to John 16:33 (ESV): *"I have said these things to you, that in Me you may have peace. In the world, you will have tribulation. But take heart; I have overcome the world."*

We shouldn't be surprised when an NFL player gets injured…and we shouldn't be caught off guard when life doesn't go exactly how we planned it would.

"Injuries" play out differently for each of us, and affect multiple areas of our lives, but we need to understand it's all part of our faith journey. We must remember that purpose and good can come from the big hits that lead to pain.

In the following verses, Paul gives us this amazing viewpoint to help alter our perspective and mindset:

Romans 8:18 (ESV) says, *"For I consider that the sufferings of this present time are not worth comparing with the glory that is to be revealed to us."*

And Romans 5:3-5 (ESV) tells us: *"More than that, we rejoice in our sufferings, knowing that suffering produces endurance, and endurance produces character, and character produces hope, and hope does not put us to shame, because God's love has been poured into our hearts through the Holy Spirit who has been given to us."*

Paul explains in 2 Corinthians 12:7-10 (NLT) that he asked God three different times to take away the thorn in his flesh (used to keep him humble), but each time God said, *"My grace is all you need. My power works best in weakness."*

Paul went on to say, *"So now I am glad to boast about my weaknesses, so that the power of Christ can work through me. That's why I take pleasure in my weaknesses, and in the insults, hardships, persecutions, and troubles that I suffer for Christ. For when I am weak, then I am strong."*

As we consider our struggles (injuries) and weaknesses, let's remember that God's grace is all we need. Let's boldly ask Him to strengthen us, so that we can suffer well for His glory.

Prayer:

Heavenly Father, I pray that my life would be filled with obedience to do Your will, even if suffering is involved. Help me to understand that when I'm weak, You have the opportunity to reveal Your power. I ask that You shine through my weaknesses. In Jesus' name, I pray, Amen.

Questions to Unpack Personally or in a Group:

1. What setbacks or "injuries" are you currently facing in life?

2. How are you handling this season of life and what are you learning about God and yourself?

3. When you look back at previous setbacks, how did God work in you and through you during those times?

4. Is it possible to view suffering as a good thing?

5. In what ways does your perspective need to change with your current situation or how do you need to change your overall view of tough situations in life?

THIS WEEK'S CHALLENGE:

Memorize one of the verses about suffering, so you are reminded God faithfully works through your difficulty.

WEEK 7

"Things will go wrong at times. Your options are to complain...or to look ahead and figure out how to make the situation better."
–Former NFL Head Coach Tony Dungy

Compounding Mistakes

As Fantasy owners, we often draft players we know we shouldn't. How many times have we drafted that older player who we've always rooted for, but deep down knew he didn't have much left in him?

Or how about that rookie running back on our favorite NFL team who we thought was going to contribute right away - even though he was still the backup?

Despite the risk, haven't we all made the mistake of taking that same player who burned us last year because we believe this season will be different?

Several weeks in, we find out the older player is too slow...the rookie running back (third on the depth chart) isn't playing...and the risky player is barely contributing, let alone scoring any touchdowns.

We find ourselves in a really tough spot because we spent a high draft pick on the veteran, and in order to justify taking him, we keep him on our roster. As a result of convincing other league members how awesome the rookie running back is, we want to prove them wrong and hang on a little longer. Unfortunately, the other risky player is just too big of a name to drop.

We don't end up admitting the mistakes we made when selecting these players and continue to stash them on our bench - even starting them during some weeks. We convince ourselves they're going to be good, but they keep letting us down over and over again. Instead of acknowledging we should never have drafted these players, to begin with, and release them, we hang on.

What we're actually doing, however, is compounding our mistakes. Instead of letting go and picking up a player on the waiver wire who could actually benefit our team, we're hurting ourselves by not moving on.

How many of us in our own lives make choices and give in to temptation when we know we shouldn't? Too often we don't stop or let go after the first mistake, so one poor move leads to another.

Convincing ourselves it's just one more drink, one more look, or one more conversation, we end up making more bad decisions. Instead of stopping the cycle and admitting we made an initial mistake, we justify our actions and continue heading down a path of compromise and compounding sin.

In Fantasy Football, when we blow it and choose a player who is hurting our team, we need to click the drop button and move on. By doing so we admit we don't want the disappointment to continue. Likewise, we don't have to prolong our misguided choices by adding more sin, but can run to the cross of Christ, receive His grace, and humbly repent.

Matthew 3:8 (NLT) says, ***"Prove by the way you live that you have repented of your sins and turned to God."***

By recognizing we're being tempted and the wrong path is in front of us, we're more likely to turn toward God before the compounding of sin begins.

James 1:14-16 (AMP) gives us insight about the steps to sin and warns us of the dangers: ***"But each one is tempted when he is dragged away, enticed and baited [to commit sin] by his own [worldly] desire (lust, passion). Then when the illicit desire has conceived, it gives birth to sin; and when sin has run its course, it gives birth to death. Do not be misled, my beloved brothers and sisters."***

1 Corinthians 10:13(NLT) offers us great encouragement when we face temptation: ***"The temptations in your life are no different from what others experience. And God is faithful. He will not allow the temptation to be more than you can stand. When you are tempted, He will show you a way out so that you can endure."***

Today as we finally release the player, let's also let go of anything in our lives that cause us to compound our mistakes. Let's decide to release the sin before it turns into more.

Prayer:

Heavenly Father, I pray You would give me the strength to resist temptation and continue to follow Your way. Help me not to turn one mistake into multiple mistakes, but understand the need to repent from my sin and rest in Your grace. In Jesus' name, I pray, Amen.

Questions to Unpack Personally or in a Group:

1. What player did you make a mistake drafting, but can't let go of?

2. In your own life, what mistake has led to another mistake?

3. Why does one sin usually end up leading to another?

4. How can you know when you're being tempted and what do you do when you are?

5. What does it mean to repent? How can you help others repent of their sin before watching them experience more pain?

THIS WEEK'S CHALLENGE:

When you feel tempted to let one bad mistake lead to another, call one of the guys in the league to ask for prayer and encouragement.

WEEK 8

Did you know?

The first Fantasy Football league had eight owners that made up the GOPPL (The Greater Oakland Professional Pigskin Prognosticators League). [5]

Counting the Cost and the Waiver Wire

One of the key ways we improve our Fantasy team is by adding a new player off the waiver wire. With a limited number of spots on our roster, there are free agents available to pick up throughout the season. Sometimes they are playing better than one of our current players or we see they have the potential to break out sometime soon and want to make sure we snag them.

Leagues set up their waiver wire differently. Some give the worst team (according to the standings) the first shot at claiming an available player, while many leagues implement FAAB to make things even more interesting. FAAB stands for Free-Agent Acquisition Budget and basically means that each owner has a certain amount of "digital" or "fake money" to use for blind bidding during the season.

Many leagues provide Fantasy owners $100 to wisely use on players we want to pick up on the waiver wire. We have to decide how much a free agent is worth and how desperately we want to have a certain player on our roster. We have to look at our budget, consider how much other owners are spending on specific positions, and then assign a value to the player we want to add.

Also as owners, we must factor in what it means to give up and release a player from our current roster in order to make room for the new guy. Ultimately, we determine if the cost for a free agent is worth more than hanging onto our auction budget and if we want to have the guy on the waiver wire more than the player on our roster.

Counting the cost as we make decisions is something we're constantly doing in our day to day life. Whether at work or at home, there is always a price to pay and a value needed to be assigned when it comes to how we spend our time and money.

Jesus invites us to follow Him and offers us the free gift of salvation. However, He warns us that we must count the cost of "picking up" our cross and "dropping" our former way of life.

Luke 14:25-32 (NLT) explains Jesus' life-changing challenge:

"A large crowd was following Jesus. He turned around and said to them, 'If you want to be My disciple, you must, by comparison, hate everyone else—your father and mother, wife and children, brothers and sisters—yes, even your own life. Otherwise, you cannot be My disciple. And if you do not carry your own cross and follow Me, you cannot be My disciple.

'But don't begin until you count the cost. For who would begin construction of a building without first calculating the cost to see if there is enough money to finish it? Otherwise, you might complete only the foundation before running out of money, and then everyone would laugh at you. They would say, 'There's the person who started that building and couldn't afford to finish it!'

'Or what king would go to war against another king without first sitting down with his counselors to discuss whether his army of 10,000 could defeat the 20,000 soldiers marching against him? And if he can't, he will send a delegation to discuss terms of peace while the enemy is still far away.'"

This is a hard passage of scripture to read, as it reveals how serious Jesus is about our commitment to Him. This isn't a casual decision we make or something to be taken lightly. While He's offering us eternal life, access to the God of the universe, and peace that surpasses all understanding, He's also calling us to value and love Him more than anything else.

In Fantasy Football, we willingly give up whatever it takes to add the players we believe in. With that in mind, let's count the cost of following Jesus and determine whether or not we're willing to give up whatever it takes to be His disciple.

Prayer:

Heavenly Father, thank you for sending Jesus to die on the cross for me. I desire to follow Him and fully surrender my life to Him. I know it might temporarily cost me on earth, but I know there's nothing more valuable than spending eternity with You. In Jesus' name, I pray, Amen.

Questions to Unpack Personally or in a Group:

1. What has been your best pickup in Fantasy or most memorable waiver wire win?

2. What stands out to you the most when you consider what Jesus said about counting the cost?

3. When it comes to following Jesus, what is the hardest thing for you to let go of? What do you lean toward loving more than Him?

4. How do you practically "carry your own cross" each day?

5. Why do you think Jesus is so serious about us understanding what it takes to be His disciple?

THIS WEEK'S CHALLENGE:

When you head to the waiver wire this week and count the cost of who you want to add, take a moment to ask God to reveal anything in Your life that you love more than Him.

WEEK 9

"I'm just trying to keep the fantasy people happy." [6] —Peyton Manning (after rushing in for touchdowns in back-to-back games)

Trying to Control the Outcome

As Fantasy Football owners, we love to take credit when our teams are winning and we put the right players in our starting lineup. We research and strategize who to play in order to give ourselves the best chance of knocking off the team we are matched up against.

When the NFL games kick off, our lineup is set and there's nothing more we can do. We place trust in the players to perform and outscore our Fantasy opponent. But when things don't go our way, it's hard not to get mad and disappointed.

Most of us intently watch the games and try to control what happens out on the field. How many times during the season do we catch ourselves yelling at the coach to run on certain plays...or we try to will the quarterback to throw to our receivers in the end zone? After all, aren't the coaches and players trying to help us win Fantasy?

Of course, there's always a reality check and we eventually realize we can't control how fast players run or how many rushing attempts they get or whether or not they get injured during the game. It's simply up to us as owners to set our lineups and accept that we've done all we can do.

In life, we also try to control the outcome of our circumstances. We attempt to entice people to do things our way and keep a tight grip on everything around us. Unfortunately, when things are out of our control and don't go according to our plan, we get anxious, impatient, disappointed, angry, and discouraged. After all, doesn't the world revolve around us?

When we start heading down this path, we must remember the words found in Philippians 4:6-7 (NLT):

"Don't worry about anything; instead, pray about everything. Tell God what you need, and thank Him for all He has done. Then you will experience God's peace, which exceeds anything we can understand. His peace will guard your hearts and minds as you live in Christ Jesus."

In order to have God's peace, we must have faith in His power and a belief that He knows what He's doing and is ultimately in control. Oftentimes we try to manipulate Him or convince Him to do things our way or in our own timing, but we can only find true freedom when we fully let go.

It's up to us to prayerfully trust and remain patient, instead of worry and be controlling. We have to remember that *"Our God is in the heavens; He does all that He pleases"* (Psalm 115:3 - ESV).

Just like in Fantasy, we do what we're capable of doing and give our best effort as we "set our lineup," but then we need to sit back and watch God move and do what He knows is best.

Proverbs 16:9 (NLT) tells us, *"We can make our plans, but the Lord determines our steps."*

Proverbs 19:21 (NLT) enforces this truth by saying, *"You can make many plans, but the Lord's purpose will prevail."*

This week, as hard as it is to let go and trust the outcome of our Fantasy matchups, let's be reminded we also control very little in life. Let's be reassured that as we place our hope and faith in Jesus, we can have peace in knowing the One who is in control will provide us the best outcome.

Prayer:

Heavenly Father, I confess that I try to control things and live in my own strength too often. Please show me how I can let go and fully trust You. I know your way is the best and I desire to have peace as I place my faith in You to do Your will. In Jesus' name, I pray, Amen.

Questions to Unpack Personally or in a Group:

1. How would you describe your viewing habits and responses when your Fantasy players are playing?

2. What areas of life do you try to control the most and have the hardest time loosening the grip?

3. Why is it so hard for you to surrender and trust that God's timing and plans are better than yours?

4. Do you recall an experience when you let go and saw God move?

5. How does believing God is in control change your perspective?

THIS WEEK'S CHALLENGE:

Ask God to show you the area of your life He wants you to let go, stop controlling, and trust Him. Then, share with another league member for accountability.

WEEK 10

"My favorite water cooler topic is Fantasy Football. I used to make fun of friends for doing it and now I'm obsessed."

–Actor John Krasinski

Admitting You're Wrong

Before Fantasy season even started, we all probably had one guy on our team who we thought would have a huge impact on our success. We hyped him up to the rest of the league and told everyone how good he was going to be. We spent a good draft pick on him and truly believed he was going to help us win.

At this point in the season, we're shocked he's been a total bust and that he hasn't contributed the way we thought he would. We've probably put him in our lineup more often than we should (even when we've known better) and have kept telling other members of the league that this was the week he was going to turn it around. Unfortunately, it still hasn't happened.

The problem is, weeks are going by and he's still on our roster, despite the harm he's causing our team (see "Week 7 - Compounding Sin"). We're too stubborn or embarrassed to admit we were wrong about him and he continues to take up a roster spot.

The best thing we can do, however, is to confess to the other owners in the league that we messed up and our analysis and predictions were misguided. We need to admit that it's time to release the player, start a fresh week with someone new, and move forward for the sake of our team.

Whether it's in Fantasy or in life, confessing to others and admitting when we blow it is very challenging. There is great difficulty in bringing to light our temptations and telling someone we've sinned. We're ashamed, embarrassed, and even stubborn about sharing our misstep...and try to hide and keep our transgressions in the dark. We don't want to concede to having a problem or let anyone know what we're struggling with.

As in Fantasy, the damage gets worse the longer we hang on without taking the necessary steps to stop the harm it's causing us. Proverbs (the book of wisdom) puts it this way in verse 28:13 (NLT): *"People who conceal their sins will not prosper, but if they confess and turn from them, they will receive mercy."*

Sometimes we think we're sneaky enough to have everyone fooled because we've hidden something about ourselves so well. But the truth is, it's eating away at us and we're much better off confessing to God and others in order for the healing to begin.

James 5:16 (AMP) says, *"Therefore, confess your sins to one another [your false steps, your offenses], and pray for one another, that you may be healed and restored. The heartfelt and persistent prayer of a righteous man (believer) can accomplish much [when put into action and made effective by God—it is dynamic and can have tremendous power]."*

God knows the truth in our hearts already, so we can come before Him with complete honesty and receive the strength we need to confess to others. In the long run, it's exhausting to live a lie and hide our struggles and secrets.

Thankfully, because of Jesus, we can rest in His love, grace, and mercy and rely on His guidance and strength to help us through restoration and repentance. As difficult as it is to admit our faults, let's allow the process of revealing to bring us tremendous healing.

Prayer:

Heavenly Father, I confess I need Your grace and forgiveness. I pray I won't hold onto sin, but instead admit when I slip up. Help me trust You for healing and restoration, and please give me the strength to rely on others to walk alongside me in this process. In Jesus' name I pray, Amen.

Questions to Unpack Personally or in a Group:

1. Which player do you still have on your roster that you need to admit was a mistake?

2. In life, what holds you back from confessing?

3. What benefits have you experienced during the process of admitting you were wrong?

4. What roles do grace and repentance play during confession?

5. Is there anything you need prayer about or something you want to confess to the league?

THIS WEEK'S CHALLENGE:

Ask God to reveal the person you need to confess to. Go to that person and admit you are in the wrong.

WEEK 11

"A winner never stops trying."

–Former Dallas Cowboys Head Coach Tom Landry

Never Giving Up

We're well over the midway point of the Fantasy season and the playoffs are right around the corner. Most likely, half our league is jockeying for a playoff position and looking to win every game down the stretch, while the other half realize it's not our year and we're fed up with our team.

By now it becomes clear which Fantasy owners have no shot at a playoff appearance because their team has only won two games. The temptation to give up intensifies as each additional loss takes its toll on owners. We don't even want to go to the league's homepage so we can avoid seeing our team at the bottom of the standings.

There's no question that losing, in general, takes a lot out of us, and in Fantasy Football it's no different. But as difficult as it is, owners are responsible to finish the season and still pay attention without walking away.

When we stop checking our lineup, leave injured guys on our roster, and never look at the waiver wire, it hurts the integrity of the league. Being matched up against a guy who checked out weeks ago may be beneficial when fighting for a playoff spot, but it also waters down the win when our opponent isn't even trying.

The best Fantasy leagues want all the owners to be active and put in the effort up until the very end. Even though there's an understanding that some teams are bad, everyone respects the guy who keeps trying different lineups and works the waiver wire to give himself a better chance to pull off an upset as the season winds down.

Whether in Fantasy or in life, our character is revealed when we face adversity, loss, disappointment, and failed expectations. We are all up against it from time to time...when everything goes wrong, when we feel we have no chance, and when unfortunate circumstances tempt us to believe our best option is to give up.

On the other hand, there are times when we feel like we're doing all the right things in life ("setting our lineup correctly"), yet injuries hit us left and right. It's during these times that we also must keep going and remember to *"...not grow weary of doing good, for in due season we will reap, if we do not give up"* (Galatians 6:9 - ESV).

Even if we lose or fail temporarily, and our circumstances are bleak, God still works in us and through us and uses it for our good and His purposes. It's up to us to keep going and *"Never be lazy, but work hard and serve the Lord enthusiastically. Rejoice in our confident hope. Be patient in trouble, and keep on praying"* (Romans 12:11-12 - NLT).

Just like the respected Fantasy leagues have owners who put in the effort all the way until the end, we reveal our commitment to Jesus and gain respect when we keep going all the way until the end.

With that in mind, let's be encouraged by 1 Corinthians 15:58 (ESV) where it says, *"Therefore, my beloved brothers, be steadfast, immovable, always abounding in the work of the Lord, knowing that in the Lord your labor is not in vain."*

Let's not give up on God or walk away and start doing our own thing. Instead, let's continue to persevere so we can proudly say, *"I have fought the good fight, I have finished the race, I have kept the faith"* (2 Timothy 4:7 - ESV).

Prayer:

Heavenly Father, I don't want to be a quitter or ever turn my back on You. I desire to trust You fully, place my hope in You, and persevere during difficult times. I ask You to please strengthen me and give me the power needed to finish strong. I pray this in Jesus' name, Amen.

Questions to Unpack Personally or in a Group:

1. Does your league agree that no owner should give up even if they're eliminated from the playoffs?

2. What disappointments in life have caused you to consider giving up?

3. What was the result of not giving up?

4. Why is it so important not to give up in life?

5. How can the rest of the league pray for you to persevere in a challenging area of your life?

THIS WEEK'S CHALLENGE:

Watch a motivational video about never giving up, such as Jimmy V's ESPY speech or a sports movie clip.

WEEK 12

"**When you have great players, playing great, well that's great football!**"

–John Madden

Hope to Make the Playoffs

An owner who is always optimistic about his team is one of my favorite types of people to play Fantasy Football with. He's the one who continues to believe his team will win and his season will turn around. At this point in Week 12, he's the one who still holds out hope that all the necessary pieces will fall into place to secure his spot in the playoffs.

Even though he has to win the rest of his games and owners with a similar record have to lose, he maintains that it will happen. Although his quarterback has to have an improbable performance and his backup running back needs a breakout game, he remains hopeful.

The reality is, Fantasy Football is wild and anything can happen. It's possible for teams to all of a sudden get hot and make a run all the way to the Championship with an underwhelming roster on paper. That's why it's crucial for Fantasy owners to keep fighting and trust that things will come together at the right time to get into the playoffs.

We know that not everyone makes it in and hope alone doesn't put stats next to our lineup, but it greatly affects our approach and mindset and how much we enjoy the last couple of games in the Fantasy regular season.

In life, it's difficult to have hope when our circumstances seem impossible to overcome. Trying to remain positive when time appears to be running out for our prayer to be answered is very challenging.

However, when we put our faith in God, there are tremendous promises available to us that provide a deep-rooted hope. Even when something appears impossible and our world is crashing in all around us, we can always cling to the truth that God is our provider, deliverer, redeemer, and restorer.

We can believe in His ability and power to come through and make anything possible. As Romans 15:13 (ESV) says, *"May the God of hope fill you with all joy and peace in believing, so that by the power of the Holy Spirit you may abound in hope."*

We are challenged in Hebrews 10:23 (ESV) to *"...hold fast the confession of our hope without wavering, for He who promised is faithful."*

Followers of Jesus live with an eternally focused hope versus a fleeting and circumstantial hope. We not only have hope that God answers our prayers and is able to fix our problems, but we have hope that He answers in a way that fits His purposes. Faith and maturity get us to this point and also allow us to continue in hope when things don't turn out exactly how we want them to.

Our true hope is found in Jesus because He makes a way for us to be saved and gives us a new life. We know our present sufferings are only temporary, so our hope propels us forward. Romans 8:23-25 (NLT) explains:

"And we believers also groan, even though we have the Holy Spirit within us as a foretaste of future glory, for we long for our bodies to be released from sin and suffering. We, too, wait with eager hope for the day when God will give us our full rights as his adopted children, including the new bodies he has promised us.

"We were given this hope when we were saved. (If we already have something, we don't need to hope for it. But if we look forward to something we don't yet have, we must wait patiently and confidently.)"

As we attempt to be optimistic and hopeful about our Fantasy team making the playoffs, let's be encouraged that lasting and genuine hope is made possible through the redeeming work of Jesus. God is able to provide whatever we need and His power continues to amaze us as we trust in Him.

Prayer:

Heavenly Father, I pray that each day I would love with great optimism and hope, knowing that You have overcome the world. Thank you for saving me and offering a way for me to know You. As I walk with You, I put my hope and trust in You, believing You can do the impossible. In Jesus' name, I pray, Amen.

Questions to Unpack Personally or in a Group:

1. Who in the league still has hope to make the playoffs?

2. What difference does being filled with optimism versus negativity make in your life?

3. What leads you to have more hope?

4. What is going on in your life that requires you to have hope?

5. What experiences from your past have you seen hope carry you through?

THIS WEEK'S CHALLENGE:

Bring optimism, positivity, and hope to those around you and let them know your hope comes from the Lord.

WEEK 13

"I'm going to come back, I can see it. It's all possible. That's why it's Fantasy. That's why you play."[7]
–Former Colts linebacker and Fantasy owner Cato June

The Player We're Glad Got Away

Before the season started, we as Fantasy owners more than likely targeted one player in particular to draft. But even though we had our sights set on making sure he ended up on our roster, there's a good chance another owner snatched him up before we had the chance.

Being one spot away in the draft order is very disappointing - especially when we're convinced the "prized player" will make our team more successful. It's easy to get mad at the owner for stealing "our guy" and beat ourselves up for missing out on drafting him.

Fast forward to week 13 and when we look back on "the player that got away," there's a good chance many of us are thankful we didn't end up with him after all. He's likely been injured on and off throughout the season or his NFL team is terrible or his production is not even close to what we thought it would be.

The player we "settled for" and drafted with the pick following "our guy," is dominating for us and has carried our team all season long. We're so glad we ended up with him and can't imagine how disappointing our season would be if we had gotten the player we initially wanted.

This sort of scenario can also happen in everyday life. Whether it's a job or promotion we think we really want...or a girlfriend we can't imagine life without...or a house we just have to have, often times we can look back with gratefulness that things turned out better than we envisioned.

At the time of the initial disappointment, we have a limited view of what's best for us or what's in store for the future. Although these are challenging situations and unfortunate circumstances that don't have the results we want, when we look back now we can clearly see how everything worked out.

The truth is, as followers of Jesus, God is working in us and through us and He's accomplishing His will by turning what we thought was bad into good.

The Bible confirms this in Romans 8:28 (AMP), "And we know [with great confidence] that God [who is deeply concerned about us] causes all things to work together [as a plan] for good for those who love God, to those who are called according to His plan and purpose."

In the Old Testament, there is a story about Joseph being sold by his brothers and thrown into a pit but later used to save his family through the power God had given him. Joseph explains to his brothers in Genesis 50:20 (AMP), "As for you, you meant evil against me, but God meant it for good in order to bring about this present outcome, that many people would be kept alive [as they are this day]."

We know pain and discouragement come when we don't get the job we want, or people reject us, or we miss out on something, or we experience some other difficulty. However, during these times when we can't believe the "player" we desired got away, we can trust that God is still good, faithful, and He's working in ways we can't always understand. Our perceived misses actually set us up for a tremendous blessing.

Prayer:

Heavenly Father, thank You for always working everything together for good. I trust Your plans and purposes are best for me, so help me be patient as I watch things play out according to Your will. In Jesus' name, I pray, Amen.

Questions to Unpack Personally or in a Group:

1. What player did you want to draft this year, but are glad you missed out on?

2. Has there been a job or situation in the past that you're thankful didn't go the way you initially wanted it to?

3. In what ways have you seen Romans 8:28 play out in your life?

4. What would it take for you to view disappointments as blessings right away instead of waiting to be thankful after everything works out?

5. How does believing the truth of Romans 8:28 change your day to day perspective on life?

THIS WEEK'S CHALLENGE:

Write down Romans 8:28 so you have access to seeing it, memorizing it, and meditating on it.

WEEK 14

"You ain't got to go home, but you got to get the heck up outta here."

–Former ESPN Anchor Stuart Scott

Fantasy Loyalty

For most leagues, week 14 is the first week of the playoffs which requires having the hottest and most reliable players in our lineup - regardless if they're a big name or not. At this point, our roster needs to be filled with players that can help us win during the next three weeks. If that means dropping one of our favorite players because he's playing poorly and likely to bring our team down, we've got to do it.

One of the keys to being a successful Fantasy owner is knowing when to be patient with a struggling player and understanding when it's time to let him go. In week 7, we discussed compounding our mistakes by hanging onto a player we shouldn't have drafted to begin with. In week 10, we brought up the importance of admitting when we're wrong about a player we hyped up.

In both cases, we are loyal to a particular player because we think he's going to be good, or we spent a high draft pick on him, or we want to show the other league members we were right, or we don't want to miss out by giving up on him too soon. There are times when patience and loyalty are needed, but in week 14, it's time to move forward with the players who are going to give us the best chance to win.

In Fantasy, it can be tough letting go of someone we've been cheering for all season, but we know it's time to make that decision. In life, there are people we surround ourselves with and friends we've known for a long time that cause us to question our loyalty. Most of the time it's great to be patient with others and stick by our friends when they're struggling.

But there eventually comes a point when we must realize they are bringing us down and their behavior is having a negative effect on us. Of course, we need to keep praying for them and let them know we still care, but we can't continue to have the same relationship we once had.

We realize that when we're around them they tempt us to act in ways we no longer want to act. We have to move forward in our lives and understand when these people aren't giving us the best chance to "win."

The Bible warns us in Proverbs 13:20 (ESV): ***"Whoever walks with the wise becomes wise, but the companion of fools will suffer harm."***

1 Corinthians 15:33 (ESV) reiterates, ***"Do not be deceived: 'Bad company ruins good morals.'"***

Loyalty is a valuable characteristic to live by, but when it causes us to keep people around who draw us away from God and invite us down the wrong path, we have to make the tough decision to go in a different direction.

Hopefully, it's only for a short season and the relationship can be restored when they're open to us lifting them up instead of them bringing us down. Walking away from the relationship may be the impetus needed to bring positive changes in their life.

The key for us, however, is being aware of the kind of people speaking into our lives and the type of impact they're having on us.

Psalm 1:1-3 (NLT) provides this encouragement: ***"Oh, the joys of those who do not follow the advice of the wicked, or stand around with sinners, or join in with mockers. But they delight in the law of the Lord, meditating on it day and night. They are like trees planted along the riverbank, bearing fruit each season. Their leaves never wither, and they prosper in all they do."***

This week let's evaluate our loyalty and make sure it's leading to victory!

Prayer:

Heavenly Father, I pray that You reveal the changes that need to be made in my relationships. Please guide me in choosing relationships that point me toward You. In Jesus' name, I pray, Amen.

Questions to Unpack Personally or in a Group:

1. What player on your roster have you been most loyal?

2. How do you know when you should remain a loyal and trustworthy friend...or walk away for a season?

3. How much of an impact do your friends have on your life?

4. What has been your experience when you've changed your relationship with certain friends because they were bringing you down?

5. What tough decisions are you facing with relationships and what action do you plan to take?

THIS WEEK'S CHALLENGE:

Ask a trustworthy league member to help you process how to navigate a friendship that you question your continued loyalty.

WEEK 15

"Mistakes are the necessary steps in the learning process; once they have served their purpose, they should be forgotten and not repeated."
—Vince Lombardi

Consequences for Bad Decisions

While some Fantasy owners are still participating in the playoffs, the rest of us are thinking back on our season and contemplating the moves we should have or shouldn't have made. With all of the decisions we're forced to make while playing Fantasy Football, the reality is we don't always make the right ones. Even so, we're still responsible for them.

We have to own up to drafting the veteran wide receiver with nothing left in his tank and the rookie quarterback who wasn't ready for the next level. We have to accept the mistake of trading for a player who had off-the-field issues and miscalculating which NFL teams would be successful this year.

We can all admit to drafting a player we know we shouldn't have or adding the wrong player from the waiver-wire when our gut feeling was to pick up someone else. These types of bad decisions cost every Fantasy owner no longer in the playoffs an opportunity at the Championship. There are consequences for making the wrong Fantasy choices.

In our own lives, we also have countless choices and unending daily decisions to make. There are temptations awaiting us and moments that will determine the path we go down. Based on what we decide, there are consequences when we make the wrong choices.

We must first decide if we want to place our hope and faith in Jesus for our salvation and receive eternal life...or face death and separation from God. Romans 6:23 (AMP) tells us, *"For the wages of sin is death, but the free gift of God [that is, His remarkable, overwhelming gift of grace to believers] is eternal life in Christ Jesus our Lord."*

Thankfully, if we place our faith in Christ, we rest in His grace and forgiveness as we seek to do His will. The consequence of our sin is no longer death, as Ephesians 1:7 (NLT) assures us that *"He is so rich in kindness and grace that He purchased our freedom with the blood of his Son and forgave our sins."*

God shows us great mercy and grace while restoring and transforming our lives, but many bad choices from our past or ones we continue to make still have consequences. We need His strength to help us face the negative effects these have on our lives.

Each day we face a decision to either follow His Word and trust His direction or pursue our own selfish desires. In order to avoid giving into sin and making foolish mistakes, as followers of Jesus, we have to constantly seek the Lord for wisdom and guidance. Moment by moment we must determine if we yield to Him or to our flesh.

If we go against what we know is right and where God is clearly leading us, we pay a price. We replace blessings, peace, and joy with unnecessary problems and emotions based on poor decisions.

Admittedly, even the owners in the Fantasy Championship make multiple mistakes along the way, but because they regularly choose the right players to put in their lineup and draft the correct guys, they now reap the benefits.

Likewise, as we desire to follow Jesus we still mess up at times. But if we truly want to do His will and stay on His path, He shows us the way to reap tremendous spiritual blessings.

With these eternal blessings in mind, let's remember the warning in Galatians 6:7-8 (NLT): ***"Don't be misled—you cannot mock the justice of God. You will always harvest what you plant. Those who live only to satisfy their own sinful nature will harvest decay and death from that sinful nature. But those who live to please the Spirit will harvest everlasting life from the Spirit."***

Prayer:

Heavenly Father, thank You for the grace and mercy You faithfully show me. Help me make wise choices so I don't have to deal with painful consequences for bad decisions. I desire to follow You and obey You. In Jesus' name, I pray, Amen.

Questions to Unpack Personally or in a Group:

1. What poor decision affected your Fantasy season the most?

2. What consequence are you having a tough time dealing with in your personal life?

3. What lifelong patterns have led you to make bad decisions?

4. What is your process for seeking God when making choices?

5. How can we help you make a wise choice today that prevents you from experiencing a bad consequence?

THIS WEEK'S CHALLENGE:

Share what you've learned from the consequences of a poor decision you once made, so that someone else can avoid similar consequences.

WEEK 16

"You got to dance with the one that brought you."
–Shania Twain

Don't Get Cute

It's Championship weekend in Fantasy Football! For the two teams competing, this is an exciting yet very stressful time. They're looking at their roster, scouring the internet for advice, stats, and analysis, and wondering which players should be put in their starting lineup. Viewed as the most important matchup of the season, there's a year's worth of bragging rights on the line.

The temptation for many owners is to overthink or second guess every lineup decision and wonder if they should bench certain players. Sometimes this includes star players who have been studs all season long but have been quieter in the last couple of weeks. They've still been winning, but they're starting to doubt how much they can trust these high-performing players. Owners may even contemplate sitting them out in favor of this week's "hot waiver wire pickups."

The best Fantasy advice in a situation like this is not to get cute, but to go with who got them to the Championship. The studs who have been reliable all season are the ones they need to play. The players who have been consistently putting up numbers throughout the year are the ones who will give them the best chance of winning. It's not worth giving up on them now and going in another direction.

In a similar way, as we follow Jesus, there will be times when He shows up in clear ways and we feel the blessings flowing through our lives. We trust Him, rely on Him, and life is really clicking. Then all of a sudden, we wonder why God is so silent. We start to doubt if He'll continue to come through and we're tempted to give up and go in another direction. We might feel like we don't want to obey Him anymore and look for something else to satisfy us.

James 1:14-15 (AMP) says, *"But each one is tempted when he is dragged away, enticed and baited [to commit sin] by his own [worldly] desire (lust, passion). Then when the illicit desire has conceived, it gives birth to sin; and when sin has run its course, it gives birth to death."*

The truth is, we have to stick with who's gotten us this far. God is almighty, powerful, loving, and our provider, and there is no reason for us to start looking to see who else is out there on the "waiver wire" or begin listening to the wrong voices.

Something might seem to temporarily satisfy us or be a better option than patiently waiting for God to come through and deliver, but nothing compares to the reliability and faithfulness of our Creator.

Even when we start to walk away from Him, He doesn't leave us and is with us in our times of need. When God commissioned Joshua, He told him this:

"Have I not commanded you? Be strong and courageous. Do not be frightened, and do not be dismayed, for the Lord your God is with you wherever you go" (Joshua 1:9 - ESV).

Not every one of us is experiencing the Fantasy Championship and making the decision on who to trust in our lineup, but each day we all choose whether or not we trust God to lead us, guide us, and provide what we need.

So when we start to doubt, look for other options, or wonder if He's still reliable, let's cling to Isaiah 41:10 (ESV): *"Fear not, for I am with you; be not dismayed, for I am your God; I will strengthen you, I will help you, I will uphold you with My righteous right hand."*

Thankfully, unlike the Fantasy Championship, victory in Christ is never in doubt.

Prayer:

Heavenly Father, I admit sometimes I doubt and wonder if You still care about me and whether or not you're still with me. In these moments I pray that I'd have the faith and strength to continue to trust You and seek You. I believe You are good and faithful, so please forgive me for looking for satisfaction anywhere else. In Jesus' name, I pray, Amen.

Questions to Unpack Personally or in a Group:

1. In the Fantasy Championship, do you agree owners should go with the players who got them there, even if they were quiet in recent weeks?

2. What situation are you having a tough time trusting God because He appears to be quiet right now?

3. What makes you start to doubt your faith or wonder if God is really there for you?

4. What are you tempted by when you think about giving up on God and going in a different direction?

5. What part of God's character do you need to be reminded of when you begin to question if He's still with you?

THIS WEEK'S CHALLENGE:

Pick a verse to memorize about God's faithfulness so it comes to mind when you start to doubt Him.

WEEK 17

"Winning isn't everything, but it beats anything that comes in second."

–Former Alabama Head Coach Paul "Bear" Bryant

Winning and Receiving Validation

After intense Fantasy drafts and 16 competitive weeks of matchups, only one champion ends the season in victory. We all start off hoping to earn the title as this year's greatest Fantasy owner, but now only one owner is admired by the rest of the league for pulling out enough wins to take home the Championship.

Up until next year's draft, this winner will feel good about proving he knew enough about Fantasy, made good roster choices overall, and did what it took to become a champion. For those of us who put a lot of effort into the Fantasy season, it's a wonderful moment when we're finally validated with a sweet win.

Being the best at Fantasy Football within our small group of friends or family is also personally affirming. When congratulated and recognized by everyone, we can't help but feel special and embrace our worth as a Fantasy owner.

In life, we all long for validation, approval, and worthiness. Whether we're working at our job...or serving at our church...or leading in our home, having our gifts and talents embraced and accepted by others is personally rewarding.

Although being a Fantasy Football winner is an awesome feeling, the validation is fleeting and next year there will more than likely be a new winner. Likewise, recognition from our boss, or compliments from a client, or appreciation from our spouse and friends are only temporary and carry limited value.

However, eternal acceptance comes when we receive God's offer of salvation. We're validated because of Jesus. We can then rest in that truth so our need for others' approval and acceptance diminish.

Romans 5:1 (NLT) says, *"Therefore, since we have been made right in God's sight by faith, we have peace with God because of what Jesus Christ our Lord has done for us."*

God's approval is what truly matters and it's important we continually make that our focus. When our priority is pleasing God above everyone else and seeking out affirmation from Him, we show our hearts are in the right place.

2 Timothy 2:15 (NLT) reminds us of this: *"Work hard so you can present yourself to God and receive His approval. Be a good worker, one who does not need to be ashamed and who correctly explains the word of truth."*

Today, let's praise God for allowing us to be accepted, welcomed, and embraced by Him because of Jesus. Let's allow that life-changing peace to give us all the confidence we need to live a life that's pleasing to Him.

Prayer:

Heavenly Father, I'm sorry I worry so much about receiving validation and acceptance from others. Help me have peace in knowing I've been made right with You because of my faith in Jesus. It's in His name, I pray, Amen.

Questions to Unpack Personally or in a Group:

1. When you won a matchup during the Fantasy season, what emotions did you feel?

2. What does your desire to win in Fantasy have to do with how you feel about yourself?

3. Why is seeking validation from the wrong places potentially dangerous to your life?

4. In what ways can you affirm and encourage another person in the league to use their gifts and talents for the Lord without the motivation of receiving applause and attention from others?

5. What session during this season of FFF had the biggest impact on you personally?

FUTURE CHALLENGE:

Continue to meet as a league during the offseason and regularly encourage each other to follow Jesus and become more like Him. Visit unpackinit.com to find more resources for sports fans.

Prayer

We pray Fantasy owners put more faith in Jesus...
than in the players on their roster.

We pray Fantasy owners have more passion about sharing the gospel...
than telling others about their Fantasy team.

We pray Fantasy owners find more joy in Christ...
than seeing their team pull out a victory in the final seconds.

We pray Fantasy owners are more committed to following Jesus...
than Fantasy stats and scores.

We pray Fantasy owners place more trust in God's Word...
than analysis from Fantasy "experts."

We pray Fantasy owners spend more time with their family and friends...
than looking on the waiver-wire to see who to pick up.

We pray Fantasy owners have peace that surpasses all understanding...
even during a losing season.

We pray Fantasy owners get angrier about injustice in the world...
than they do about the best player on their roster getting injured.

We pray Fantasy owners believe God is a God of miracles...
even beyond hoping for a dramatic comeback during Monday Night
Football to win their matchup.

We pray Fantasy owners embrace real winning...
as receiving God's grace and forgiveness.

In Jesus' Name we play and pray...AMEN!

The Top Fantasy Football Player to Own Each Season from 2004-2017 According to FFF [8]

2004: Daunte Culpepper, Quarterback, Minnesota Vikings - 5,123 total yards

2005: Shaun Alexander, Running Back, Seattle Seahawks - 27 rushing touchdowns

2006: LaDainian Tomlinson, Running Back, San Diego Chargers - 31 total touchdowns

2007: Tom Brady, Quarterback, New England Patriots - 52 total touchdowns

2008: DeAngelo Williams, Running Back, Carolina Panthers - 1,636 total yards

2009: Chris Johnson, Running Back, Tennessee Titans - 2,509 total yards

2010: Arian Foster, Running Back, Houston Texans - 2,220 total yards

2011: Aaron Rodgers, Quarterback, Green Bay Packers - 4,643 passing yards

2012: Adrian Peterson, Running Back, Minnesota Vikings - 2,314 total yards

2013: Peyton Manning, Quarterback, Denver Broncos - 56 total touchdowns

2014: Le'Veon Bell, Running Back, Pittsburgh Steelers - 2,215 total yards

2015: Antonio Brown, Wide Receiver, Pittsburgh Steelers - 136 receptions

2016: David Johnson, Running Back, Arizona Cardinals - 2,118 total yards

2017: Todd Gurley, Running Back, Los Angeles Rams - 2,093 total yards

UNPACK this...

Make more of your day by taking a 2-Minute Timeout to read a complimentary weekday devotional email/blog from UNPACKIN' it Ministries. Sports fans are encouraged and challenged to follow Jesus as we unpack one of the day's top stories and relate it to our own lives. Each day's devotional focuses on a relevant Bible verse and closes with a short payer. You'll be inspired and will want to continue to unpack the topics throughout your busy day.

SUBSCRIBE NOW AT
unpackinit.com/Subscribe

Through this popular Bible reading app, UNPACKIN' it Ministries offers various 5-day reading plans that unpack sports stories along with Biblical Truth. Through a lens of faith, you'll be challenged, encouraged, and inspired as a fan to follow Jesus and become more like Him.

Simply download the YouVersion app on your mobile device and search for "UNPACKIN' it."

UNPACK FAITH & SPORTS BY LISTENING IN

Join Bryce Johnson as he unpacks sports, faith, and life with intruiging guests from the sports and entertainment world. Subscribe to the podcast and/or tune into the nationally syndicated radio show to hear a freshly unpacked message each week.

THE UNPACKIN' it PODCAST
with Bryce Johnson

Subscribe using your favorite podcast source or visit
unpackinit.com/podcast

Airing on radio stations across the country each week.
unpackinit.com/radio

UNPACKIN' it
Sports Fans Following Jesus

References

1. https://www.sbnation.com/ad/16119954/explainer-nfl-fantasy-football-history

2. https://www.mercurynews.com/2015/09/13/fantasy-football-was-born-in-oakland-original-league-still-thriving/

3. http://www.espn.com/nfl/columns/story?columnist=garber_greg&id=2684942

4. https://amp.usatoday.com/story/sports/nfl/steelers/2013/07/27/troy-polamalu-pittsburgh-steelers-training-camp/2592941/

5. http://www.nfl.com/fantasyfootball/story/09000d5d80021ece/printable/fantasy-football-101

6. http://www.espn.com/nfl/columns/story?columnist=garber_greg&id=2684942

7. http://www.espn.com/nfl/columns/story?columnist%3Dgarber_greg%26id%3D2684942&sa=D&ust=1534863501350000&usg=AFQjCNH7rtCQB3crbWFqxO7BArxfh9n-gA

8. https://www.pro-football-reference.com and
https://sports.gunaxin.com/50-greatest-fantasy-football-seasons-nfl-history/200921

CPSIA information can be obtained
at www.ICGtesting.com
Printed in the USA
BVHW09s1823130918
527388BV00010B/86/P